This journal belongs to:

_____

WHY ARE WE INSIDE A CLOUD?

An Activity Journal to Ease Flight Anxiety

By Ariela Rudy Zaltzman and Cecilia Santini

CHRONICLE BOOKS
SAN FRANCISCO

ISBN 978-1-7972-1482-5

MIX
Paper | Supporting responsible forestry
FSC™ C008047
FSC
www.fsc.org

Manufactured in China.

Design by Evelyn Furuta.
Illustrations by Maggie Chiang.

10 9 8 7 6 5 4 3 2 1

CHRONICLE BOOKS
680 SECOND STREET
SAN FRANCISCO, CA 94107
WWW.CHRONICLEBOOKS.COM

TABLE OF CONTENTS

INTRODUCTION

You don't like flying. We don't like flying. It's why you're here; welcome, this book is for you.

While venting about our mutual fear of the equal parts terrifying and astonishing reality that is flying, we realized flight lovers often try to comfort anxious fliers by listing all the facts and statistics about the safety and technology of airplanes. They try to use logic to fight emotions. In one such instance we were told, "You know, you really shouldn't worry about turbulence—it doesn't mean the plane is falling; it probably just means we're going through a cloud." And that sparked a flash of realization: While flight lovers might relish the science behind the miracle of human flight, we flight haters (yes, we know *hate* is a strong word, but sometimes it's accurate) recognize just how ridiculously wild it is that we could even *be* inside a cloud—and if you think about it, it's hard not to question ourselves. Why are we even doing this? Why are we subjecting ourselves to this unnatural, biology-defying, gravity-ignoring situation? After all, there's a reason we weren't born with wings.

We are giving up control of our destinies for the duration of the flight as our lives are placed in the hands of a disembodied voice speaking over an intercom (possibly telling bad pilot jokes). We are forced to confront our mortality, while being subjected to the whims and personalities of strangers who might—dear God— want to speak to us.

When faced with such nightmarish scenarios, perhaps frantically drawing some sheep will ease your pain (pages 19–21). Maybe taking comfort in familiarizing yourself with those around you (page 32) will help you escape the cage of your own mind. Will dreaming up an entire blockbuster franchise (pages 79–82) distract you from the turbulence? You will find these and other activities and questions throughout this book, waiting for you to lay your anxious burdens at their goofy feet.

We discovered that laughter helped us through our own flight anxiety, and we wanted to share a little bit of that with you, so this journal is silly. It doesn't feature wellness exercises or meditation practices; there are many apps and other books for that. (If you feel like reflecting on your ability to love yourself, there is some freewriting space throughout.) This journal will hopefully make you smile, inspire some creativity, cause some eye rolling, and take you to happier places than a cramped metal tube hurtling through the sky.

Much love, fellow traveler. It will all be okay, probably.

—Ariela & Cecilia

FLYING WORDS AROUND THE WORLD

Use your travels as a way of learning new languages! Ask the people you meet to help you fill in a column with their country's language, or fill it in yourself by observing the signs, publications, and advertisements around you.

ENGLISH			
Hello			
Hotel			
Bathroom			
Airport			
Fly			
Terminal			
Passport			
Luggage			
Water			
Food			
Cloud			
Please			
Thank you			

PREFLIGHT CHECKLIST

★ Boarding pass

★ ID (and/or passport)

★ Luggage tag

★ Phone and phone charger

★ Headphones

★ Petty cash

★ Hand sanitizer

★ Water bottle to fill up once you're through security

★ Snacks

★ Tissues

★ Novel that you would only ever read in an airport (there is no shame in airports)

★ Pen

★ Pillow/Blanket

★ Eye mask

★ Earplugs

★ Extra pair of socks

(Reminder: Carry-on liquids are limited to 3.4 ounces [100 ml] per container.)

TAKEOFF

WELCOME TO YOUR SEAT!

Acquaint yourself with your surroundings. Make sure your belongings are organized—take out your cell phone, headphones, water bottle, book/tablet, and a pen, and put it all in the backseat pocket for easy access throughout the flight. Take a look around. Where's the nearest bathroom? Look for the flight attendants so you know who they are in case you need them at any time.

If you could have one superpower, what would it be and what would your superhero name be? Draw your outfit.

SUPERPOWER _____

SUPERHERO NAME _____

OUTFIT

Describe or draw a place that makes you happy, whether it's your home or a café or a park.

Draw as many sheep as you can while the plane takes off.

SAMPLE

Draw as many sheep as you can while the plane takes off.

SAMPLE

Draw as many sheep as you can while the plane takes off.

SAMPLE

QUIZ TIME!
WHAT KIND OF ANXIOUS FLYER ARE YOU?

What is your least favorite part of flying?

- **A.** Flying!!!!
- **B.** Going through security
- **C.** Listening to other people's phone calls at the gate

What do you dread most once you're in the air?

- **A.** Death
- **B.** Having to go to the bathroom
- **C.** My seatmates speaking to me

When do you feel the most relief?

- **A.** When the plane lands
- **B.** When I get my luggage from baggage claim
- **C.** When the person sitting next to me puts headphones on and closes their eyes

What is your ideal flight distraction?

- **A.** There is no escape, only temporary relief
- **B.** Making a to-do list
- **C.** My tunes or a novel

Who would you rather have as your seatmate?

A. A spiritual figure to guide my soul to its rest

B. A frequent flier who can give me tips, airline ratings, and educational flying stories

C. Emptiness

If you answered mostly A, you are an existentially anxious flyer. You fear death. It's okay, though—we all do. Perhaps an impromptu imaginary therapy session might help? Check out page 154.

If you answered mostly B, you are a logistically anxious flyer. What if your luggage is lost? What if your seatmate falls asleep and you can't get up to use the bathroom? Check out the activity on page 35 to ease some of your planning worries once you land.

If you answered mostly C, you are a socially anxious flyer. Your worst nightmare is a chatty seatmate. Consult the activity on page 26 for contingency plans should such a terrifying scenario occur.

If you could have one unusual talent that is almost but not quite a superpower (e.g., the ability to always find a clean bathroom whenever you need it), what would it be?

CONNECT THE DOTS

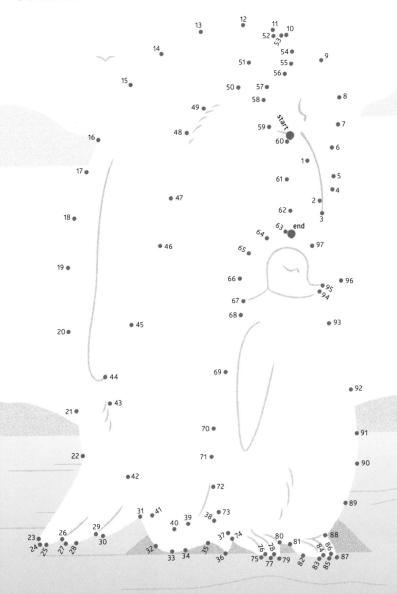

Make up a fake autobiography to have ready if a stranger talks to you.

_____

_____

_____

_____

_____

_____

_____

_____

_____

_____

_____

_____

_____

_____

_____

_____

_____

_____

Describe the perfect airline, run by you.

_____

_____

_____

_____

_____

_____

_____

_____

_____

_____

_____

_____

_____

_____

_____

_____

_____

_____

_____

BINGO

A TYPO	A CRYING BABY	SOMEONE TALKING ON THE PHONE	A COUPLE IN LOVE	A LANGUAGE YOU DON'T UNDERSTAND
SOMEONE WEARING A SLEEP MASK	SOMEONE GOING TO THE RESTROOM A LOT	A HARDCOVER BOOK	SOMEONE WITH A FLASHY NAIL COLOR	TWO PEOPLE WEARING THE SAME HEADPHONES
A SUNSET	A HALF-COMPLETE CROSSWORD PUZZLE/SUDOKU		A PERFUME AD	SOMEONE PLAYING GAMES ON THEIR PHONE
SOMEONE USING A LAPTOP	A PAIR OF HIGH HEELS	SOCKS ON FEET (NO SHOES)	CHEWING GUM	SOMEONE SNORING
A PET	A SPILLED DRINK	A PREGNANT PERSON	SPORTS ATTIRE	SOMEONE SNIFFLING

CONNECT THE DOTS

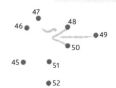

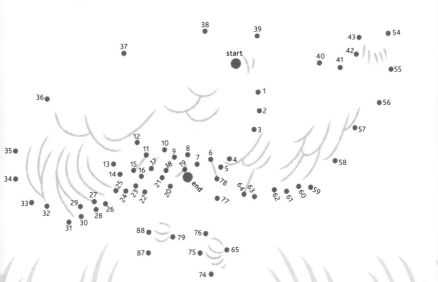

If you could sit next to any famous person, living or dead, who would it be? Imagine your conversation.

31

Observe your fellow passengers. Try to predict which ones will hop up as soon as the plane lands and which ones will wait patiently for the plane to taxi to its arrival gate.

Find a cute pet picture on your phone and draw a portrait of them here.

Write a checklist of your to-dos when you arrive at your destination and for your return flight (if you like thinking that far ahead).

- [ ] _____
- [ ] _____
- [ ] _____
- [ ] _____
- [ ] _____
- [ ] _____
- [ ] _____
- [ ] _____
- [ ] _____
- [ ] _____
- [ ] _____
- [ ] _____
- [ ] _____
- [ ] _____
- [ ] _____
- [ ] _____

Turbulence is caused by a sudden change in airflow, which can be a result of hot air rising from the clouds, the plane's own jet streams, or mountains in the surrounding landscape that distort the windflow.

FREE DRAWING/WRITING SPACE

Round windows' lack of sharp corners helps balance out the stress levels from the pressure difference between the outside and the inside of the plane as it goes higher up into the sky. Be like a round window and let your stress go!

The average commercial airliner flies between 31,000 and 38,000 feet, varying by aircraft, although their service ceiling, or the maximum altitude they're certified to fly at, is higher. The higher a plane flies, the thinner the air, and the less resistance the plane encounters.

IN FLIGHT

WELCOME TO THE AIR!

Time to release all that nervous energy.
When it's safe to do so, unbuckle your seat
belt and walk around the cabin. Use the
bathroom if you need it, then return to
your seat and take a look out the window.
Most importantly: Remember to breathe.

Do you remember the first time you ever flew? Who was with you and where were you going?

_____

_____

_____

_____

_____

_____

_____

_____

_____

_____

_____

_____

_____

_____

_____

_____

_____

Draw a short comic. Optional title: *The Flight of the Manatee.*

COMIC TITLE

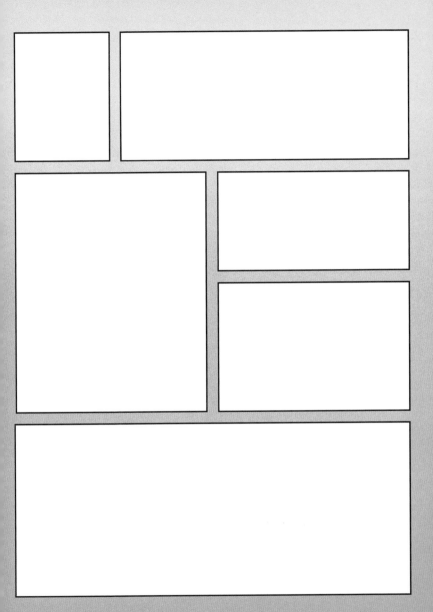

49

Write a story about a person you spot on the plane.

_____

_____

_____

_____

_____

_____

_____

_____

_____

_____

_____

_____

_____

_____

_____

_____

_____

_____

_____

_____

How long is this flight? What else could you accomplish in this amount of time? For example, how many *Lord of the Rings* movies could you watch?

FLIGHT LENGTH:

ACTIVITY:

FLIGHT LENGTH:

ACTIVITY:

FLIGHT LENGTH:

ACTIVITY:

FLIGHT LENGTH:

ACTIVITY:

FLIGHT LENGTH:

ACTIVITY:

Write a story about a bug trapped in an airplane.

What was your favorite music at different times in your life?

TIME IN YOUR LIFE:

MUSIC:

TIME IN YOUR LIFE:

MUSIC:

TIME IN YOUR LIFE:

MUSIC:

TIME IN YOUR LIFE:

MUSIC:

TIME IN YOUR LIFE:

MUSIC:

TIME IN YOUR LIFE:

MUSIC:

Make a playlist for your next flight.

★ _____
★ _____
★ _____
★ _____
★ _____
★ _____
★ _____
★ _____
★ _____
★ _____
★ _____
★ _____
★ _____
★ _____
★ _____
★ _____

Make a playlist for someone you care about.

★ _____

★ _____

★ _____

★ _____

★ _____

★ _____

★ _____

★ _____

★ _____

★ _____

★ _____

★ _____

★ _____

★ _____

★ _____

★ _____

Everyone has loved at least one TV show that had a terrible ending. Now is your chance to fix it.

Write a review of the last book you read.

BOOK TITLE:

RATING: ✈ ✈ ✈ ✈ ✈

_____

_____

_____

_____

_____

_____

_____

_____

_____

_____

_____

_____

_____

_____

_____

_____

_____

Write a review of the last movie you watched.

MOVIE TITLE:

RATING:

If there were a town named after you, what would the flag look like? What would the local food be? What would the climate be like? What would some of the street names be?

LOCAL FOOD:

CLIMATE:

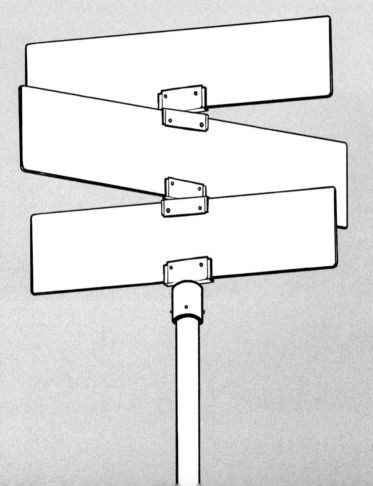

SOME JOKES

Tell them to your seatmates... if you dare! Then write your own joke.

If a seagull flies over the sea, does a bagel fly over the bay?

How do you make a tissue dance?
You put a boogie in it!

Did you know the first French fries weren't actually cooked in France?
They were cooked in Greece.

I'm reading a book about antigravity.
It's impossible to put down.

What noise does a 747 make when it bounces?
Boeing, Boeing, Boeing.

What did Tennessee?
The same thing that Arkansas.

What did the drummer call her twin daughters?
Anna One! Anna Two!

How do celebrities stay cool?
They have many fans.

Why can't you hear a pterodactyl go to the bathroom?
Because the p is silent.

Two guys walk into a bar . . .
the third one ducks.

Why did the coach go to the bank?
To get her quarterback.

YOUR JOKE:

Write a song using the following words: *peach, owl, aperitif, gold.*

What's the first memory you have? If you're not sure, make one up.

_____

_____

_____

_____

_____

_____

_____

_____

_____

_____

_____

_____

_____

Practice your drawing skills. Try copying an image you like from a page in the in-flight magazine.

AUTOGRAPH LOG

If you don't want to ask people for their autographs, imagine what their names are and what their signatures might look like.

_____
Pilot

_____
Flight attendant

_____
First officer

_____
Best-dressed person
on the plane

_____
Stranger closest to you

_____
Person who looks the
happiest to be there

_____
Person who looks the least
happy to be there

_____
A first-time flier
(After you land, there is a 42%
chance a flight attendant will joke
that it's the pilot.)

Sketch what you see in the clouds out the window.

WORD SEARCH

D	E	S	T	I	N	A	T	I	O	N	C	A	D	H
Z	M	H	S	G	J	Y	W	W	Y	T	Z	L	N	N
T	V	B	I	L	C	O	D	U	Q	G	C	T	Y	J
L	E	E	D	M	E	F	U	J	O	R	N	I	F	N
M	L	N	A	I	Z	Z	U	R	U	U	J	T	K	S
S	T	S	G	N	I	W	T	I	N	S	C	U	N	E
X	O	O	O	I	E	E	S	E	A	E	I	D	G	I
G	H	S	L	U	N	I	E	G	R	B	Y	E	S	K
A	P	E	N	P	N	E	G	C	P	P	C	D	K	O
E	R	W	I	G	E	N	A	U	E	T	U	Y	A	O
F	N	L	S	E	B	F	R	T	C	O	Y	X	J	C
I	O	R	F	I	Q	Z	E	K	L	T	U	W	O	K
T	D	F	X	I	S	R	V	C	T	N	E	C	S	A
A	O	Z	E	G	R	I	E	G	K	G	U	R	C	H
C	I	I	X	G	H	U	B	J	W	I	N	V	B	G

Altitude	Coffee	Destination	Pilot
Ascent	Cookies	Engine	Pretzels
Beverages	Cruising	Journey	Wings
Clouds			

CONNECT THE DOTS

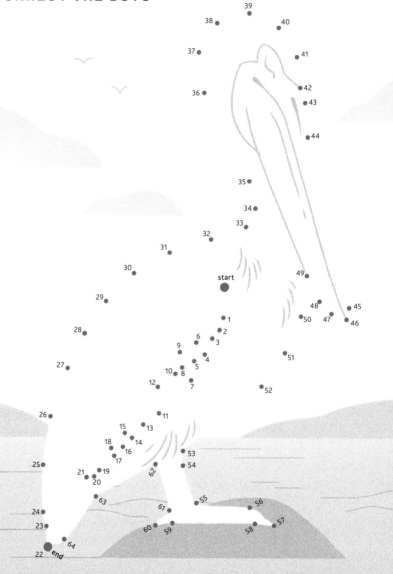

LABEL THE DIAGRAM

Do you know what all the gadgets in a cockpit are for? Neither do we.* Take a guess here if you like, then turn the page for a closer look at the cockpit.

*But thankfully the pilots do! They rack up thousands of hours of training and flight experience before flying for commercial airlines.

AIRPLANE COCKPIT

Altitude Indicator

Direction Finder

Primary Flight Display

Rudder/Brake Pedals and Footrests

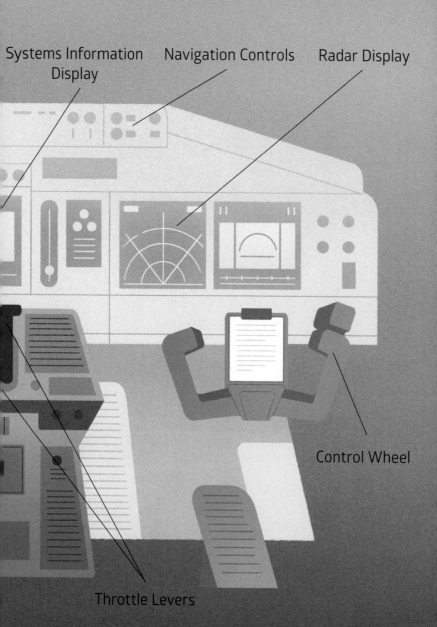

Systems Information Display

Navigation Controls

Radar Display

Control Wheel

Throttle Levers

Think of all the movies you've seen that take place in airplanes. If you want, pick five words that describe how each movie makes you feel.

MOVIE TITLE:

RATING:

KEYWORDS:

MOVIE TITLE:

RATING:

KEYWORDS:

MOVIE TITLE:

RATING:

KEYWORDS:

MOVIE TITLE:

RATING:

KEYWORDS:

MOVIE TITLE:

RATING: ✈ ✈ ✈ ✈ ✈

KEYWORDS:

MOVIE TITLE:

RATING: ✈ ✈ ✈ ✈ ✈

KEYWORDS:

MOVIE TITLE:

RATING: ✈ ✈ ✈ ✈ ✈

KEYWORDS:

MOVIE TITLE:

RATING: ✈ ✈ ✈ ✈ ✈

KEYWORDS:

Rank airplane snacks and drinks from best (10) to worst (0).

NAME	RATING	NOTES

Come up with a movie plot that takes place in an airplane.

Come up with a sequel movie plot.

The Sequel

_____

_____

_____

_____

_____

_____

_____

_____

_____

_____

_____

_____

_____

_____

_____

_____

Come up with a conclusion to your epic airplane movie trilogy.

The End

Design the poster for your blockbuster movie series.

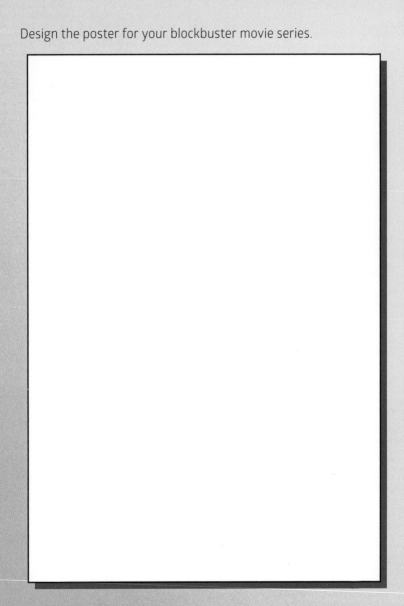

Focus on deep breathing, and shade in one sheep per breath.

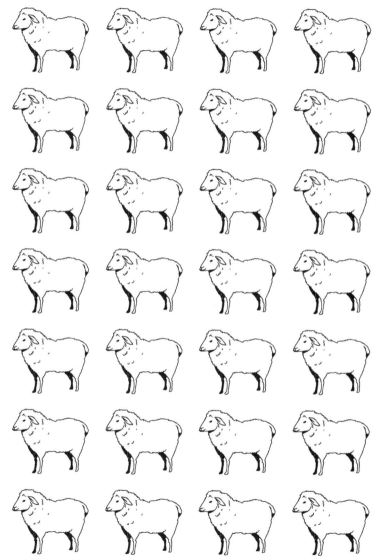

WORD SEARCH

S	O	X	P	G	G	V	Y	O	I	H	O	A	M	C
A	Y	Q	U	U	N	T	O	V	F	S	V	J	A	Y
S	H	O	E	S	I	S	C	G	Q	E	E	R	Y	Z
T	B	E	Z	R	D	L	E	V	L	U	R	D	O	O
K	Y	G	U	W	R	R	U	S	U	Y	H	H	W	L
L	J	C	L	O	A	F	I	G	O	M	E	X	O	R
H	E	D	K	R	O	A	F	N	G	G	A	C	D	M
S	Y	M	U	W	B	U	T	O	B	A	D	P	N	U
S	K	C	A	N	S	U	E	T	E	J	G	I	I	Q
S	L	E	E	P	L	K	C	B	B	K	V	E	W	K
H	X	D	V	L	C	V	O	K	C	X	A	N	L	T
V	Z	H	P	W	C	I	A	S	L	B	P	T	W	A
Z	I	Q	T	Q	F	H	K	B	V	E	Z	N	H	U
K	X	R	T	A	F	Z	K	J	Y	S	L	Y	D	P
C	H	S	W	O	E	Y	K	W	N	U	W	D	I	F

Aisle	Carry On	Security	Snacks
Boarding	Luggage	Shoes	Takeoff
Buckle	Overhead	Sleep	Window

Draw or describe your ideal airplane meal (drink included!).

Make up a recipe for your ideal plane drink and give it a suitably aeronautical name.

DRINK NAME

If you could pick a travel buddy (person or pet) for a trip, who would it be and why? (If you're already flying with someone, you don't have to tell them about this.)

TRIP:	FROM		TO
DATE		BUDDY	

TRIP:	FROM		TO
DATE		BUDDY	

TRIP:	FROM		TO
DATE		BUDDY	

TRIP:	FROM		TO
DATE		BUDDY	

What can you do on a plane or at an airport that would be weird if you did it anywhere else?

_____

_____

_____

_____

_____

_____

_____

_____

_____

_____

_____

_____

_____

_____

_____

_____

_____

_____

_____

Plan your perfect trip. Where are you going? For how long? With who? How will you get there? What kind of place are you staying in? Will it be a relaxing vacation on the beach or a touristy adventure full of museum visits? What is one concrete action you can take now or when you arrive at your destination to make sure you can make this dream a reality?

_____

_____

_____

_____

_____

_____

_____

_____

_____

_____

_____

_____

_____

_____

_____

_____

_____

List three to five acts of kindness you could do right now for those around you.

★ _____

★ _____

★ _____

★ _____

★ _____

Imagine a miniseries is being made about your life. Pick the director, writer, and cast. What is the climax of the story, and how is it resolved?

Director:

Writer:

Cast:

Climax and resolution:

You're not alone! Draw or make a list of other things that can also be inside a cloud (e.g., a balloon that got away, birds, San Francisco on a foggy day, rockets on their way to space).

Write a note to yourself ten years from now.

If you were to write an autobiography, what would you call it? Draft an opening paragraph.

TITLE: _____

_____

_____

_____

_____

_____

_____

_____

_____

_____

_____

_____

_____

_____

_____

If you could do one thing knowing for sure that you would be successful at it, what would you do?

What's the nicest thing anyone has ever done for you? Write a thank-you letter. (If you feel so inclined, share it with them when you next see them.)

_____

_____

_____

_____

_____

_____

_____

_____

_____

_____

_____

_____

_____

_____

_____

_____

Design your own pair of shoes.

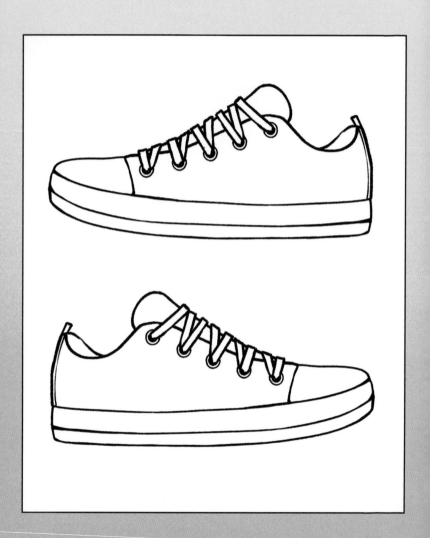

How would you have gotten to your destination four hundred years ago?

_____

_____

_____

_____

_____

_____

_____

How would you get to your destination four hundred years in the future?

_____

_____

_____

_____

_____

_____

_____

TIC-TAC-TOE!

(If you are flying solo and don't feel like talking to strangers, save this for your next flight with a travel companion.)

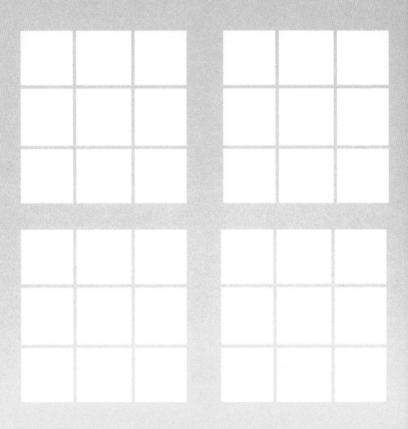

Practice your haiku skills. Remember, three lines: five syllables for the first, seven syllables for the second, and five syllables for the third.

_____

_____

_____

_____

_____

_____

_____

_____

_____

_____

_____

_____

_____

DOTS AND BOXES GAME

(If you are flying solo and don't feel like talking to strangers, save this for your next flight with a travel companion.) Take turns drawing either a vertical or horizontal line that connects two points. Whoever completes a square writes their initial inside it and gets another turn. The player with the most squares at the end of the game wins.

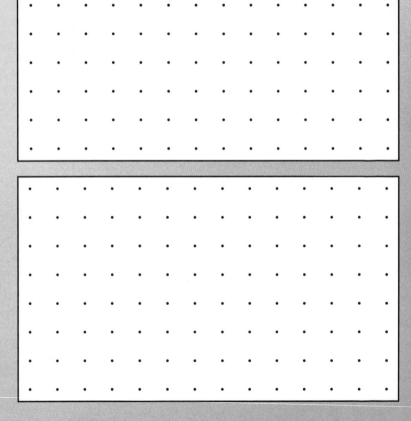

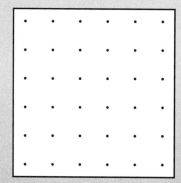

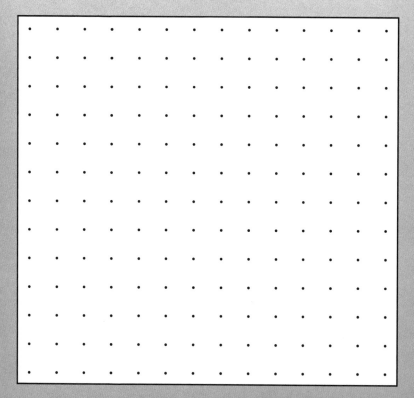

Imagine going back in time and explaining planes to Sacagawea.

FREE DRAWING/WRITING SPACE

Commercial airline pilots always file flight plans with the airport's air traffic control tower at least half an hour before the plane is scheduled to leave its gate. The flight plan includes the airplane model, the airspeed and cruising altitude, the route of the flight, and the destination airport. The air traffic control tower approves the flight plan and creates a data log (called a flight progress strip) with important information about the flight that is then passed between air traffic controllers along the route.

There isn't a clear etymology for the term *cockpit*. One explanation traces the term to cockfighting, while another points to a nautical term for the spot on ships where the coxswain, who was in charge of steering, was located.

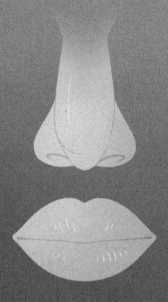

When we're flying tens of thousands of feet in the air, our senses of taste and smell are affected. Low air pressure lowers our taste buds' sensitivity to salty and sweet foods. And the extreme dryness of the air inside the plane prevents our scent receptors from working properly, making us less sensitive to smells.

According to calculations made in 2017 by flight data company FlightAware, on average there are over 1 million people in the air at a given time. Exact estimates vary based on the data sources, but it's safe to say that at any moment, there are hundreds of thousands of people in the sky.

LANDING

FAREWELL TO THE SKIES!

We know it wasn't easy, but we're proud of you for getting this far.
As the plane prepares for landing, clear the clutter in your mind by clearing the clutter around you. Hand your trash to the flight attendants, take a sip of water, and make sure your belongings are organized. This will help speed up the process of deboarding so you can get to your destination ASAP.

Make a list of things you're excited to do when you get to your destination. (Remember, you can use this journal during different flights.)

★ _____

★ _____

★ _____

★ _____

★ _____

★ _____

★ _____

★ _____

★ _____

★ _____

★ _____

★ _____

★ _____

★ _____

★ _____

★ _____

Make a list of things you're excited to do when you get to your destination.

★ _____

★ _____

★ _____

★ _____

★ _____

★ _____

★ _____

★ _____

★ _____

★ _____

★ _____

★ _____

★ _____

★ _____

★ _____

★ _____

Make a list of things you're excited to do when you get to
your destination.

★ _____

★ _____

★ _____

★ _____

★ _____

★ _____

★ _____

★ _____

★ _____

★ _____

★ _____

★ _____

★ _____

★ _____

★ _____

★ _____

What is something about the future that you're excited for?

Draw as many sheep as you can while the plane descends.

SAMPLE

Draw as many sheep as you can while the plane descends.

SAMPLE

Draw as many sheep as you can while the plane descends.

SAMPLE

Draw as many sheep as you can while the plane descends.

SAMPLE

Return to your passenger behavior predictions on page 32.
How did you do?

_____

_____

_____

_____

_____

_____

_____

_____

_____

_____

_____

_____

_____

_____

_____

_____

_____

Write your name in as many different ways as you can think of.

If you could make up a holiday, what would it be, and when and how would it be celebrated?

_____

_____

_____

_____

_____

_____

_____

_____

_____

_____

_____

_____

_____

_____

_____

_____

_____

_____

_____

Imagine your fellow passengers as sea creatures, and sketch or describe them.

Imagine your fellow passengers as sea creatures, and sketch or describe them.

Pretend this journal is a therapist. Tell it your fears. Where do they come from? How does that make you feel?

Go back in time to a past flight when you were scared. Tell your past self that the plane landed safely and it all turned out okay!

_____

_____

_____

_____

_____

_____

_____

_____

_____

_____

_____

_____

_____

_____

_____

_____

_____

_____

Two Boeing 747s were used to piggyback 83-ton space shuttles across the United States, and even once internationally. The planes were called NASA 905 and NASA 911, and they ferried shuttles that landed in California back to launch facilities in Florida. You can visit one of these airplanes, topped with a full-size space shuttle replica, at the Johnson Space Center in Houston, Texas.

Draw what you imagine an airport on another planet would look like.

FREE DRAWING/WRITING SPACE

Although airplanes are designed with multiple engines for optimal performance, it is possible to safely perform an emergency landing with just one engine.

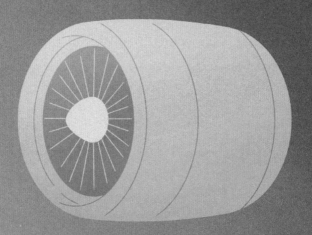

A Boeing 737 can hold between 6,800 and 7,000 gallons of fuel. If a regular car (with a fuel efficiency of 30 mpg) could hold that amount of gas, it would be able to drive around the equator (24,901 miles) approximately 8.5 times.

OVERHEARDS

Write down interesting/funny/quirky/confusing "overheards" from the pilot, the crew, or other passengers.

FREE DRAWING/WRITING SPACE

FLIGHT LOG

Date:	Airline / flight no.	Departure point:	Destination:	Aircraft:	Distance traveled:

NOTES:

Date:	Airline / flight no.	Departure point:	Destination:	Aircraft:	Distance traveled:

NOTES: _____

_____
_____

Date:	Airline / flight no.	Departure point:	Destination:	Aircraft:	Distance traveled:

NOTES: _____

_____

_____

Word search solution for page 70 (first puzzle)

D	E	S	T	I	N	A	T	I	O	N	C	A	D	H
Z	M	H	S	G	J	Y	W	W	Y	T	Z	L	N	N
T	V	B	I	L	C	O	D	U	Q	G	C	T	Y	J
L	E	E	D	M	E	F	U	J	O	R	N	I	F	N
M	L	N	A	I	Z	Z	U	R	U	U	J	T	K	S
S	T	S	G	N	I	W	T	I	N	S	C	U	N	E
X	O	O	O	I	E	E	S	E	A	E	I	D	G	I
G	H	S	L	U	N	I	E	G	R	B	Y	E	S	K
A	P	E	N	P	N	E	G	C	P	P	C	D	K	O
E	R	W	I	G	E	N	A	U	E	T	U	Y	A	O
F	N	L	S	E	B	F	R	T	C	O	Y	X	J	C
I	O	R	F	I	Q	Z	E	K	L	T	U	W	O	K
T	D	F	X	I	S	R	V	C	T	N	E	C	S	A
A	O	Z	E	G	R	I	E	G	K	G	U	R	C	H
C	I	I	X	G	H	U	B	J	W	I	N	V	B	G

Word search solution for page 84 (second puzzle)

S	O	X	P	G	G	V	Y	O	I	H	O	A	M	C
A	Y	Q	U	U	N	T	O	V	F	S	V	J	A	Y
S	H	O	E	S	I	S	C	G	Q	E	E	R	Y	Z
T	B	E	Z	R	D	L	E	V	L	U	R	D	O	O
K	Y	G	U	W	R	R	U	S	U	Y	H	H	W	L
L	J	C	L	O	A	F	I	G	O	M	E	X	O	R
H	E	D	K	R	O	A	F	N	G	G	A	C	D	M
S	Y	M	U	W	B	U	T	O	B	A	D	P	N	U
S	K	C	A	N	S	U	E	T	E	J	G	I	I	Q
S	L	E	E	P	L	K	C	B	B	K	V	E	W	K
H	X	D	V	L	C	V	O	K	C	X	A	N	L	T
V	Z	H	P	W	C	I	A	S	L	B	P	T	W	A
Z	I	Q	T	Q	F	H	K	B	V	E	Z	N	H	U
K	X	R	T	A	F	Z	K	J	Y	S	L	Y	D	P
C	H	S	W	O	E	Y	K	W	N	U	W	D	I	F